Jesus a Mere Image?

Roisin Rzeznik

Jesus a Mere Image?

Copyright © 2012 Roisin Rzeznik

Copyright © 2004 Roisin Rzeznik

All rights reserved.

ISBN:0615607802
ISBN-13:978-0615607801

Dedicated to:
My Savior; My Light, My Refuge, My Rock, My Strength, My Rainbow, My Friend, My Hero, My Lord, MY EVERYTHING!!!!!!!!!!!!

-Roisin

CONTENTS

Acknowledgments	i
Beautiful	1
A Heart Like His	2
May We Never Be Apart	3
Day After Day	4
Thank You	5
You	6
My Father	7
Faraway	8
Dance	10
I Look to You	11
Life	12
Future	13
Jesus is in Control	14
To My Love	16
Christmas Gifts	17
Peace	18
Missing You	19

The Magic Dance	20
Beyond The End of Time	21
From Nowhere	23
Everyday-A Prayer for a Friend	24
Secret Love	25
No One	26
On Bent Knees	27
Your Will-Never Quit	28
Never	29
Cry	30
December Night	31
Love	32
Divine	33
He	34
Word to a Friend	35
Message of Love	36
Jesus	37
Let It Snow	38
Play: Note to a Friend	39
Rejoice	40

Jesus a Mere Image?

Reprinted for Joe Elliott; in loving memory of Joe Sr.

© 2004 Samuelson; Christmas Gifts
© 2004 Samuelson; The Magic Dance
© 2003 Oppermann; Never
© 2003 Oppermann; Cry

Used by permission

Jesus a Mere Image?

ACKNOWLEDGMENTS

Thank you to all of my beautiful children for their love and heartfelt contributions to my world and Jesus a Mere Image…

My sweet grandbaby

Joe

My Grandmothers, Grandfathers, and Uncle Paul for their love, patience, and kindness.

"Anam Chara, Domani è oggi…Amore Eterno"

My Extended family, whom love at all times…

You know who you are!

"Thank You"
Jesus

The Tolerant Twilight Singers

Bobby Sands

"The Woman Cried"

Jesus a Mere Image?

BEAUTIFUL

Lord, You are beautiful like Spring flowers in full bloom

You are so beautiful when I feel your touch
I know You love me very much

More beautiful than the butterfly
You light upon my heart and wipe the tears from my eyes

You are so beautiful you've shown me how to be free

You're more precious than the finest tea

Thank you for loving me

A HEART LIKE HIS - A LONELY PLEA

Silently I plead for your salvation-
I pray to my Lord
I ask Him to arm you with far more than
a sword
I beg His protection for you day and
night-
I pray that He will continue to hold you
upright
For far too long I've endured this pain
I can't even shake the thoughts of you
As I walk through the cold rain
I pray Jesus leads you where you need to
go-
I'll never cease prayer for you
I love you so
I know all will be well in time
I can't wait to see you climb
There is no need for worry at the Lord's
side-
Oh how glorious the changing tide

MAY WE NEVER BE APART

Love-Love-Love from above
It's a truth I've never felt before-
Jesus the One and Only
Love-Love-Love the Lord has opened the door
Jesus, Keeper of my heart
Redeemer of my soul
Love-Love-Love like never before
Jesus the One I adore
Love- true love as precious as a snow white dove-
The Lord Jesus is pure and true
Love-Love-Love love sent from above
like nothing you've ever experienced before
Once you've felt it you'll want more

DAY AFTER DAY

Lord- My Dear Lord
You- leave me breathless
What can I say
You- sharpen my senses
Day- after day
Just when I think
I can't go on…
Another day-Another minute
Your love shines on me
Again and Again
As it lights the way
Day-after day

THANK YOU!!!

Faith is a funny little word
no doubt
It's not as complicated as it seems
Once you figure it out
you'll say
It's a funny little thing
To feel
Alive again
Oh-Lord
Thank You for
Mercy, grace, and faith
But
Most of all
Thank You for being You
A Friend to the end
A true message of love You send

YOU

You saved me
No measure for the love
You gave me
Strength to carry on
You restored me
Better than ever before
Love for evermore

MY FATHER

My Father
He brings me the very best
He loves me
He bestows His love
No match found
None among the rest
He delights in me
He makes me smile
My Father
He is a man called Jesus
He has style!!!!

FARAWAY

I can't help but wonder how faraway you
are
I stare at each passing car
I gaze at the moon
I wonder if I will see you soon
I know that thought is but a dream
A cost not too high
A small price
Ah, to know you've been redeemed
So I sit and I cry
I wipe the tears from my eyes
There is so much we take for granted
This world we live in has become so slanted
I love you
I know somehow you love me too
If things would have been different would
we care…
would we love this deeply

Jesus a Mere Image?

would we share
Our every moment
Our every thought
Our every prayer
Oh, how I long for you to be here
But I know you must be there
What keeps me going is knowing
The Lord is near
God is by your side
All things are possible
All things for you He will provide
When we meet again
There will be no need to pretend
Our love will last
We'll move forward without a past
Every moment will be savored
No, not artificially flavored
No need then, to wonder how faraway
When the time comes our love will stay
No need to wonder how faraway

DANCE

This is a love that is going to last
This kind of love happens so fast
It's a sweet romance
Entwined in an endless dance
This is a love without end
I need no promises to know
Wherever I am you go
A carpenter's hands
The detailed plans
The love just grows and grows
With You there is no fear
No foes
I've discovered Heaven on Earth
In the form of a Man
Let Him touch your heart
You will understand
This is a love that is going to last
This kind of love happened so fast
It's a sweet romance
Enjoy the endless dance

I LOOK TO YOU

I look to You like a child
Often I feel like a newborn
Clumsily in the newness my legs wobble
I cry for You
As I make my way
Into Your outstretched arms

LIFE

Today
Yesterday
Seems so faraway
Yesterday
Today
Wasn't even a dream
Imagine

FUTURE

Your touch is like no other
You are always there for me
More faithful than a brother
I never dreamed life could be this way
I found a home with You
I am so happy
You had me stay
I count my blessings as days go by
I look to the future
Tears of joy flood my eyes
I never want to leave this place
I want it to last forever
An everlasting grace

JESUS IS IN CONTROL

Do you still remember
Feel the love we share
It's only in this world of chaos we're kept apart
At times it seems we could never be more alone
When you see the truth and see the light
You'll see we're not alone
We're on our way home
I beg you
Take my hand and join me on the walk home
We're almost home
Yesterday it seemed our only hope lay in dreams
I feared dreams alone could not sustain us
I was afraid we'd never reach home again
I love you
My heart cries out for you daily
Jesus
Jesus gets me through
His love fulfills me
It will never fail me
His love for us comes shining through
You'll see it's true
It won't be long now

Before he brings me back to you
He's leading us through
Through the rain
Opening doors
Removing our pain
Take my hand

And join me
Take His hand
He is leading you back to me
He is ready to set us free
So together in love we can walk home with Jesus
Jesus, Jesus
Leading us through the dark
Jesus, Jesus, Jesus
Reuniting us
It's Jesus
Jesus, Jesus
Jesus is Love
Jesus is understanding
Jesus, Jesus, Jesus
He is leading me back to you
Jesus! Jesus! Jesus!
Thank You!!!!!!

TO MY LOVE

My love I miss you!!!!!!
I'm so blue without you!
Do you know it's true?
I believe in you!
I believe in You!!
My hope is in the Lord!
My trust is in the Lord!
I know you love me too!
Together we'll see each other through
There is no distance too far
Let's bridge this gap
Let's cover the scar
Let's heal the pain
Our hope is in the Lord!
Put your trust in the Lord!
Where thoughts and dreams remain
Together we're walking with Jesus!!!!

CHRISTMAS GIFTS

BY
JEFFREY J. & ROISIN

Christmas time
A delightful time of year
The festive lights reflecting on the fresh blankets of crystals
Joy filling and dancing in our hearts
Hope enveloping our minds
Fear is dispelled with no place to go
Anxiously awaiting the arrival of treasured gifts
Eyes young and old sparkle like rainbows of diamonds and colorful gems
Cherubs' kisses on children's cheeks
Glee's notes resonating on the crisp cool air
Skaters gliding like eagles on mirrors of ice
Warm embraces from a long lost friend
These are the cherished gifts from our Lord

PEACE

What about peace
Have we forgotten
Does anyone care
Do we see what's going on
Why is everyone losing their hair
Has anyone stopped to wonder
We just keep running at warp speed
There's something in the air
Listen closely
It's a direction we should all heed
Listen closely
Let the voice lead

PEACE…

MISSING YOU

Longing, waiting, caring…crying
Hoping, praying, saying…repeating
Sighing, dying inside…
Staying, going, lost without knowing…
Missing him
More and more everyday
Lord keep me from being so blue…
I've no one but You!!!
In You, I find my comfort
Easing my pain
Stopping the internal rain
Lost without You…

THE MAGIC DANCE

BY
JEFFREY J. & ROISIN

Midnight sparkle dances on the desolate road like hidden
diamonds in the dust
The darkness is illuminated by the tender
Moonbeams
The magic of dancing is a must
Love entwined figures
Dancing with the One you can trust
The magic dance

BEYOND THE END OF TIME

Tell me, do you feel it too?
What is this connection I feel with you?
It's love…the truth you feel is love…

Like a dream…
You've wandered gracefully into my life…

But where is hope when you're filled with strife

Do we find the love of a lifetime
And walk on by…

How can it be…
Can we pass and just sigh…
Tell me, you'll at least whisper, "Hi!"

How many more years…
Do I have to fight back these tears…

To live without you…again, is to die…

Without the promise of You
I wouldn't even try…To carry on

To carry on…to carry on

A lonesome task…

Please, please don't ask me to stay behind the
Mask…
If it's true and you feel it too
Don't walk on by
I beg you, don't leave me here to cry…to die…
Again
I love you more today than I ever could have
yesterday…
the years haven't washed away the love…the
pain…
Everything still remains…
Memories don't fade in time…
That heart you hold in your hand is mine…
It's yours now and forever…
Beyond the end of time…

FROM NOWHERE

Curiosity turns to concern
Concern to caring
Alarm turns to worry
Now I sit here and wonder
I pray you're still there
In this night full of thunder
I don't know who you are
Which rock was I under
Where did you come from
From nowhere, you've landed in my life
You are here to add to my life
Things…
Things I've never had before
A love to open a door
And so much more
A hand to gather roses
Tell me you're Rose's
A man to fill the spaces
In me…
There are so many places
To be touched
Oh, to be loved so much…

Roisin Rzeznik

EVERYDAY-A PRAYER FOR A FRIEND

Everyday-Everyday
I long for you
Wishing you well
There's nothing more to tell
No better words to say
I pray-I pray
Everyday
For you to be okay
For you to walk back into my life
For you to succeed
For the Lord to fulfill your every need
I need…
you now
So much
More than I needed you then
This time let's not pretend
Because
I know I love you
I know what I feel
What I feel is real
This love makes it quite easy
To kneel
I love you so
So much
Wisdom in the truth
I pray soon I'll hear you say it too
Promise you'll never let me go
I love you, …

SECRET LOVE

Secret Love inside my soul
The music plays such a sweet melody
Secret Love You've made me whole
I reached out
You offered Your hand
You said, "Follow Me!"
"If your love is true you'll lay it all down…"
There was no demand
I gave not a second thought
No reason
With that…
My Secret Love set me free
I was no longer lost, but found
I discovered things I'd never sought
I learned things I never knew could be thought
Sown with love
Blanketed in passion
A pure delight
My Secret Love
My Rescuer in the night
Never again will I lose sight
Of what can be
Nor will I forget
The joy of being free
Secret Love residing in my heart…lover of my soul
Thank You for loving me!
Thank You for making me whole!!!
I will walk with you through eternity!!!!
Thank you for loving me!
Thank You!!!

NO ONE

Life moving slower than I want it to
There were so many times
I could have truly used a friend
In those times
I found no one
No one to care
No one who could understand
You alone can see
You alone understand
You are the One living inside of me
Tell me Friend because I need to know
I'm not sure which way to go
I'll hold your hand
Guide me fair
Even when there's no one else who will care
I know You are always there
I love You more than life itself
There is no one who can compare
Nothing and no one can compete with the love we share

ON BENT KNEES

I bow before You
On bent knees
You are my Delight
The Love of my life
I long for the day that I become Your wife

I bow before you
On bent Knees
I adore you
The love of my life
I long for the day that I take you as my wife

Together forevermore
On that day we will celebrate
The beginning of our life
The husband and the wife
A love without strife

YOUR WILL-NEVER QUIT

Lord You never quit
When I thought all was lost
When I had no way home
You were there for me
Lord I will never quit
You saved
You gave
All when You could have left me
Instead You promised me
As long as I have breath
I will never quit
Your will is my only desire
Just when I think things could never be better
You take me higher

NEVER

BY
STEPHANNIE AND KATHRYN

I never want the world to end
Just take a walk with me my friend
First look at the stars
Then you'll see why the world shouldn't end
I don't want the world to end
I just want the stars to shine
Find peace in your mind
And look to the love in your heart
It helps me find peace
It will help you find peace in your mind

CRY

BY
KATHRYN

I do not want to die or cry
I just want to live my life
In paradise
My life is turning blue
Just because I lost you
I just want to cry
But I might die
I am on a bended knee
Begging you to come back to me

DECEMBER NIGHT

December coming to a close
The wind carries a chill
A short walk leaves frigid toes
The crispness of the air
Entices one to get their fill
The evening sky is dark and fair
The stars shimmer in the still
I can feel Him on the calming breeze
His voice whispers in the wind
I hear Him calling, calling
Blowing through my hair
Caressing my face
In my ear whispering
Murmuring, "Friend…"
Peace and Love is the message He sends

LOVE

To man
Love is like no other earthly thing known
To the ears
Its music is a sweet and soothing sound
It is hard to give understanding
To something so misunderstood and
unknown
Love is stronger than death or anything else
earthbound
It can be harsh enough to knock a king from
his thrown
Love can even make one wail like a hound
It is the most wonderful thing the Lord has
ever sown
Love can be literally heaven on earth
Yet gone wrong
It can leave your heart to bleed upon
Crimson splattered ground

DIVINE

To live is divine, but
To pass into the divine is a dream of
Mine…
Someday it will be realized
Until then please be my friend…
Most days it isn't easy
Hard to believe He won't leave me

HE

He will never leave me…
He has led me to freedom
With His love I have become me again
When you look at me what do you see
I cannot repay Him there is no worldly sum
He will forever be my Best Friend
And the One and Only to which I always run
Jesus, He has freed us…

WORD TO A FRIEND

A word to a Dear Friend
This message of love I do send
I love You more today than ever before
Time spent with You makes me crave more
Just the thought of You brightens my day
How my heart feels for You there are no words to say
This heart You have put on the mend
A message of love my Dear Friend
Friends 'til the end

MESSAGE OF LOVE

"Message of love"
"Message of love"
Listen to the sweet sad song
"Where has He gone"
"He is gone"
Rings through the air
Sunrise so beautiful
Wondrously beautiful
Hues begin to awake
Painting the sky
Vibrantly dancing across the sky
Colors
All the elegance can't mask the cry
"I miss my Love" is the cry
Painful memories and broken dreams
Bittersweet cries
Mourning doves and butterflies

JESUS

Joy
Excellence
Sweet Devotion
Unbridled Love
Secret Passion

LET IT SNOW

Let it snow
Let's go
Run through the fields
Slide down the hills
Lie in its depths
Spreading our wings
As the pristine wind sings
Crystals of heaven fall upon our faces
Looking up wide-eyed
Distant time and places
How small we truly are

PLAY: NOTE TO A FRIEND

You are my friend
I love you for all you do
This is for you
I love you more today than yesterday
I love to see you play
Watching you-I wonder
Will you play today
I can see you smile- run- laugh-
As if a child
What does it take to have such grace
To be: So liberated- So free
Precious, rare and as delicate as lace
Don't ever leave me alone in this place
Forever I want to dance with you
Laugh with you- Walk with you- Talk with
You
I just want to be with you…Please stay
Friend, I could go on forever and a day…
Instead take my hand let's play
Wouldn't you rather just play

REJOICE

Love me
Now and forever
Never let me go
I'm waiting for you
Tell me you love me so
(It's been) So long since I've seen your face
I wonder how I'll ever survive this fate
Oh Lord, please reassure me-
It's never too late…
For a man to change his ways
Lengthen his days
I long to hear your voice
If you were near…
Oh, if you were here- I'd beg you
I'd beg you- "Sing praise-sing praise"
Then together we'll rejoice
Rejoice for you've made the right choice

Jesus a ~~Mirror~~ Mere Image?

Or

A Living God!

ABOUT THE AUTHOR

Roisin Rzeznik

Roisin Rzeznik is best known by her pseudonym Roisin (Van gogh-Rzeznik). She is a Midwest, Milwaukee, Chicago area artist, writer, photographer, pragmatic philosopher, activist, and humanitarian. She has four children whom are now grown and a grandson.

She enjoys creating....

Roisin is a versatile artist working with many mediums and experimental techniques...most prevalent are her paintings and an occasional block print or rare drawing. Her focus is on contemporary art, abstract expressionism, research, visual rhyme, and poetry.

A tremendous lover of the archaic, prose, and art world-wide. The artist was inspired at an early age by her mentors and their willingness to indulge, experiment, and instruct in a broad, diverse, and eclectic range of art, technique, and philosophy.

Over the years Roisin has spent her time highlighting Fair Trade, fighting for human rights, women's rights, children's rights, racial congruity, the abolition of extreme poverty, Aids, Malaria, human trafficking, and Genocide.

Roisin is known for often crediting her greatest loves as influences including God Himself; music as her muse and those whom create it.

Roisin credits Greg Dulli as the magical masterful genius whom constantly drives her to explore her artistic direction and often fill page upon page with verse. Of which, Filthy Sleaze (Out Damn Spot), her latest poem, which is said to illuminate the darkness surrounding human trafficking and other global and societal ills has been compared to Allen Ginsberg's Howl.

Roisin harbors a deep belief that, "Global Peace and Unity are achievable; They are a tangible gift from the Almighty."

www.ingramcontent.com/pod-product-compliance
Lightning Source LLC
Chambersburg PA
CBHW071801040426
42446CB00012B/2660